XYZ PUZZLES AND OTHER STORIES

AF518119

DEVAN VETTATH

Clever Fox®
PUBLISHING

Chennai • Bangalore

CLEVER FOX PUBLISHING
Chennai, India

Published by CLEVER FOX PUBLISHING 2025
Copyright © Devan Vettath 2025

All Rights Reserved.
ISBN: 978-93-6707-184-7

This book has been published with all reasonable efforts taken to make the material error-free after the consent of the author. No part of this book shall be used, reproduced in any manner whatsoever without written permission from the author, except in the case of brief quotations embodied in critical articles and reviews.

The Author of this book is solely responsible and liable for its content including but not limited to the views, representations, descriptions, statements, information, opinions and references ["Content"]. The Content of this book shall not constitute or be construed or deemed to reflect the opinion or expression of the Publisher or Editor. Neither the Publisher nor Editor endorse or approve the Content of this book or guarantee the reliability, accuracy or completeness of the Content published herein and do not make any representations or warranties of any kind, express or implied, including but not limited to the implied warranties of merchantability, fitness for a particular purpose. The Publisher and Editor shall not be liable whatsoever for any errors, omissions, whether such errors or omissions result from negligence, accident, or any other cause or claims for loss or damages of any kind, including without limitation, indirect or consequential loss or damage arising out of use, inability to use, or about the reliability, accuracy or sufficiency of the information contained in this book.

FORWARD

On fourth of April 1959, I opened my eyes and ears to the world around me and from then on what I have seen, heard and observed remains as impressions in my mind. At times I feel it embarrassing that more than sixty years of life I lived in this planet could not obliterate the impressions. This is my earnest effort to offload some of the memories and the history of the village where I was born laced in fiction. Though I feel it a relief akin to someone feeling a lesser weight on his head after shedding a substantial part of burden, I am clueless about how the readers will accept it. Since a lucid style of writing is not adopted deliberately about which I am still apologetic, it is to maintain the intensity of emotions and situations. Rather than a single reading, a repeated reading may elucidate and benefit in getting a clear picture and provoke the thoughts of the reader. Apart from the impressions everything else that one would find while reading the stories including the characters are fictitious and has nothing to do with anybody living or dead. If somebody finds some similarities with any of the characters it is only coincidence which I cannot help. I only wanted to reveal the social settings and moorings recorded for the generations to come.

This book is a collection of seven stories with titles; Homage, The XYZ Puzzles, The Bridge, The Island of Neurotics, The Fall of a King, Corporate Holiday and The Journey Begins. The stories weave around human emotions, confusions and mundane human relations. Some glimpses of the matrilineal system of life prevailed in a community in Kerala can be seen in the story, "the fall of a king". The aspirations, trials and tribulations of the people of a village is depicted in the story, "The Bridge". The story," The Journey begins" gives some psychological insights into the married life past middle age. Other stories delve on inter-personal relations in day-to-day life in office and society.

AUTHOR BIOGRAPHY

Born in 1959 in the still obscure village Melmuri at the western end of Palakkad district in Kerala, South India. Father Karunakaran Nambiar was the head master of the primary school in the village and mother Kalliani kutty Amma was a housewife. They are no more. Father expired in 2016 and mother in 2021 leaving behind the author and his two siblings, a sister and brother. After lower primary education in the village school successfully completed the school education in Janatha High School in the neighbouring village Naduvattom. Then studied for the pre-degree course at the government college, Pattambi and for bachelor's degree in Physics at N.S.S.College, Ottappalam both in Palakkad district and under Calicut University. After graduation worked for a brief period as quality control chemist in a chemical factory in Mumbai. Then left the job to join the Accounts and Finance department of Southern Railway in 1983. Retired as senior section officer (Finance) in 2019 and stays in Palakkad. Wife Sujatha is working in the divisional head quarters of Southern Railway in Palakkad. Their daughter is a bank employee in Chennai, son in law an IT Professional and son a pediatrician in Palakkad. Post retirement he has acquired an additional qualification as communication English trainer. Besides his interest in reading and travel he has been an ardent practitioner of reiki who can vouch for its healing power showing a long list of patients healed.

BOOK DESCRIPTION

XYZ PUZZLES AND OTHER STORIES is a collection of seven short stories. In a nut shell, the stories weave around human feelings and emotions in mundane life, spread over office and domestic environments. The social settings and moorings of many bygone decades happening around locations in south India can be seen recorded in the stories.

While bittersweet memories are depicted in "HOMAGE," friendship withered away has been narrated in the title story, "THE XYZ PUZZLES". The inner turmoil suffered silently by men is depicted in the stories, THE ISLAND OF NEUROTICS, CORPORATE HOLIDAY and "THE JOURNEY BEGINS". The aspirations and struggles of a village for electricity and a bridge connecting them to main land and the fulfilment of such desires, half a century ago is the centre point of the story, "THE BRIDGE". Some glimpses of the matrilineal system of life prevailed in Kerala can be traced in the story, "THE FALL OF A KING".

CONTENTS

HOMAGE

The road from the airport was busy with vehicles carrying passengers and their relatives. Through the dissipating morning mist what caught his attention was the neon sign board at the far end, "RENT A CAR". Sooner a new idea flashed his mind to hire a car and drive straight to his destination instead of going to the railway station. For the destination, he had no clear idea about it yet, though he had told his wife Sarika that he was leaving for his native place. The word native place from his mouth was much to her astonishment than disbelief that it was the first time he was talking about it in the twenty years of their courtship. She knew very well that his life has been replanted in Mumbai just after university education somewhere in Kerala. Since she belonged to Sangli in Maharashtra she was quite unaware of place names in Kerala except for one or two towns like Cochin and "Tribandrum". What she couldn't understand was his new like for native place after so many years." I will tell you everything after my return," he told her.

From the very moment of receiving the message he was in frantic search in whole Mumbai city for a rose flower. Though it was available everywhere in various hues, he wanted one with the natural rose shade and fragrance. He hated the tissue-cultured, grafted or budded available in all colour combinations. Those were synthetic to him, not much different from plastic flowers vexatious to butterflies. When reminded or chided that you are the leading Indian manufacturer of formaldehyde, the raw material for plastics, he would retort, "it is my livelihood. It is the only job and trade I know. Still, I advise people to use green teak wood leaves or dry plantain leaves for wrapping food stuff and the like and paper bags in place of polythene pickups.

Finally, he got it and there were no limits to his ecstasy when a Sardarji, a tanker lorry driver working for his company brought one, with a one-foot-long stem and a few leaves. Its fragrance filled the whole mansion prompting Sarika to comment, "Oh Lord, such things are grown on earth!" "Ha maji……Andheri me rehnewala ek railway officer ki bagiche se mila. Yeh phool market me milnewala nahi." [Yes, madam, I got it from a railway officer's garden in Andheri. This flower is not available in market.]

He had no time to waste lest the flower would be taken off its fragrance, freshness and hue by time. So did he take the midnight flight from Mumbai to Coimbatore and from there rented the car and drove to his destination. Though he liked driving, all his cars were chauffeur driven. Hence seldom drove his own cars. Now the window glasses down, he felt the morning breeze gently traversing the upper part of his body. It must be two hours' drive, he worked out in his mind. The beeline of lorries carrying straw, some with head lights still glowing coming across from opposite side did not irritate him nor did those hurrying up over stepping the lane to overtake other vehicles and pounce in front, frighten him.

Past the check post at Walayar, more than a score of small towns he might have sailed, all familiar by name. Now crossed his home town too, he did not know where to go next, as things, buildings, places everything tangible have changed a lot. He pulled up near a mango tree and a tile roofed building which stood unchanged but for the growth of the tree. The road map to his destination was gradually unfolding in his mind. Guided by the map he began to walk towards the stream ahead to cross it and continue his journey on foot when a stranger told him that there is a bridge a few meters away. Back in the car he continued to drive past the bridge.

Now he is in front of the lower primary school where learnt the Malayalam alphabets from Kunjukutty teacher in first standard and English alphabets from Karunakaran master while in class four. In between Narayanan master taught in class two and Poduval master in class three. Madhavan master was in charge of class four. Karunakaran master adorned the office of headmaster also. Then there was only one building, long with tiled roof and class rooms and office room partitioned with bamboo screens. Later with the surge in the number of students necessity of additional divisions and class rooms arose. But to accommodate the students of a new division the space in the existing building fell short miserably. Though an additional division brings with it the fortune of an additional post of teacher the school managers were an unfortunate community those days. New appointments did not fetch huge money to the managers then. With the meagre grant from government, they were struggling even to meet the expenditure for minor repairs of the building and benches. However pressure was built on the manager C.K.Menon overtly and covertly from all corners to which he could never yield because it was absolutely beyond his fiscal means. So, he shrugged off such suggestions in the most characteristic hesitant mood possible.

This background prompted the headmaster Karunakaran Nambiar to form a committee of the villagers to mobilize public opinion and funds for the noble cause. Though in general terms it may be a noble cause it turned out to be a dream project for the headmaster that he got fully immersed in it and sweated blood to get it finished. He was seen riding and roaming pillion on the contractor's motor cycle to ensure the quality of materials being procured for the construction. Donation coupons were printed for collecting money. Some receipt books were sent beyond the borders of the state and the country. While the whole world rallied behind the dream only one person found something sinister in entrusting a receipt book to his son in law working in north India. He intervened to bring back the book without collecting a single paise and returned it to the headmaster with rebukes. Starting from first standard every year a new division was added for four years with an additional appointment of four teachers. Meantime the school was taken over by a man from Gulf at a time the tides were changing and the fortunes tilted in his favour to reap the harvest.

Parking the car under the tree in front of the school compound, he turned to the alley towards the right. It was a working day for the school. From the thatched shed attached to the high-rise side wall between the alley and the school compound, smoke billowed in the air and the smell of boiling rice permeated the area.

Many a picture flashed through his mind, the sweet smell of yellow-coloured uppuma, the vegetable oil can, milk powder in polythene pouches, everything supplied by C.A.R.E, the American relief agency and the native cook Appunny Nair.

The body was placed on the floor of a tiny hall for receiving the last respects. He made way through the squatting women around the body and nipped the flower from the thorny stem, bent forward to place it just above her heart. A loose petal from the flower drifted in the air. He stood there with closed eyes and clasped hands for a moment. His mind was tracking the loose petal. He could see a young lady sitting on a door step, a pendant gold coin resting on her abdomen where the saree had been shifted aside by the blowing wind. The drifting petal gradually moved downwards and was just to settle on her body. He opened his eyes........the pendant gold coin was not there.....the rose petal had taken its place. He felt relieved as if a window threw open and the room filled with air and light.

THE XYZ PUZZLES

They stood on either side of the road, facing each other with an air of confoundation whether to smile or not. The road was stretching out from east to west. At the western end the sun was sinking gradually in the Arabian sea. They did not smile nor did they raise their hands to say "hello". Minutes before in the convention center where they attended the wedding reception of the son of a common friend, only providence would have prevented them from a close encounter. Now there are many possibilities including the natural course of both of them hurrying up to cross the road to come closer and eventually shake hands at the middle of the road creating a chaotic traffic jam. As well they can depart and disappear into the oblivion as x and y. Indeed, they were meeting eye to eye after so many years. Old friends they were somewhere else on the globe.

Long back it was a time when men and women named A, B, C, D.... toiled with pen, paper, type writer and comptometer in offices and hundred c. c. bikes like IND-SUSUKI, HERO HONDA, YAMAHA, and KAWASAKI

BAJAJ were not on the roads. LAMBY, LAMBRETA and VIJAY SUPER were commoners against the aristocratic BAJAJ CHETAK. In that period of transition from single groups to double income groups a few couples were seen moving out on scooters at the stroke of five from office. Young and eligible bachelors vied one another for courting the newly appointed sari-clad, most of whom owed their job to their deceased father while in service.

In the world of A to Z there were only a few bachelors and spinsters.

The married ones rushed to their homes or quarters at the stroke of five or even before that, in case such a golden chance befall. Only bachelors or those living single as their wife and children are left in their native place used to hang out and among them were X and Y.

X had some oddities of character and behavior as noticed by Y at the first instance he saw him in flesh and blood. But it did not arise any surprise as he had received some hints about it from some other sources beforehand. The mystery about him was in fact increasing as he had been absent from duty for a few weeks and just turned up that day. While introducing each other, though it was a known fact that both are unmarried Y wanted to know more about the other's family. So, he asked, "what about father, mother, and siblings"? Curt, came the reply from X, which was rather evasive, "I have everybody at home". There was a hidden message in reply. Realizing that he could not insist further, Y just nodded his head in acceptance of the reply and his right for privacy. Sometimes one longs for a friend at one's side, that was Y'S predicament. However, he found something congenial in X which matched well with PAUL VALERY's categorization of minds. According to the French poet and essayist there are three types of minds, great minds, average minds and small minds, where great minds discuss ideas, average minds discuss events, and small minds discusses people. Unostentatiously they discussed art, culture, music, cinema, literature, sports, national and international politics. Literally they couldn't afford any time for petty office gossips.

Amidst the progress of the friendship what surprised and dismayed Y was the latent longing in X for praise and accolades. Wherever available he accepted it without any qualm or shame even if it originally belonged to some other person. The first time he noticed it was, when the office superintendent M praised him for the prompt and fastidious conduct of a tea party in office. Though he had no role in organizing it and the credit should go to another person X never tried to correct M but shook hands thanking him with a sepulchral smile which he passed on to Y also followed by a wink. Behind the glee the craving for admiration and applause was visible. Often it appeared that his behavior smacked of snobbery rather than the scholastic vibe expected from him. Even then he got along well with all class of people, maintained close company only with a few distinguished persons whom he ensured were professionals in their respective field. But he never failed to greet with a hello and smile at those he would meet every day in and around his office. In fact, his rich play of words fascinated them to him. However, he was afraid of revealing his true nature to the outside world as if wanted to be shrouded in some mystery. As far as possible he tried to keep others away and remained aloof.

X and Y maintained a friendship which included an occasional drink of beer and short-term borrowing of small amounts of money by X from Y. The purpose of the soft loan was never a topic of discussion between them, but Y had observed the habit of the other man receiving the loan by right hand repaying it by left hand. After a few instances Y commented about it in a lighter vein to which he replied that, "I am deft with both hands and both are sacrosanct to me, no taboo for the left." Nevertheless, X reminded the need of maintaining the secrecy about such deeds in view of the circle of other friends enjoyed by Y. He was very much worried about maintaining his image as a teetotaler though both had such an image undisputed. As he was of marriageable age according to the socio-cultural conditions of the area it was usual to face questions regarding marriage from all corners which he used to shrug off in a devious manner. Later he will open up his mind to Y regarding marriage and his indecisiveness and lack of confidence about it. At that time Y who was four years younger to him was seriously in the lookout for a suitable life partner. By now a close friend, he sought the help of none other than X to post a matrimonial advertisement in a weekly magazine in the latter's address and scrutiny the mails in response. Breaking his record of abstentions of marriage and other social functions X attended the marriage also leading to comments from other office staff.

Like all others X also desired to procure a scooter and thought that it would be better to acquire cycle balance before that and bought a bicycle. After a few days of serious effort to learn cycling he gradually felt disenchanted not only with cycling but with the cycle itself. To his solace fortune appeared in the form of the store boy to take over the cycle on easy instalments, which he never paid except for a few initial instalments. Now his attention diverts to the departmental promotion examination which he had skipped during the past many years. Once he was equipped with all departmental code books and manuals and a non-departmental easy chair to prepare for the first chance of the examination. The voluminousness of the books began to disenchant him after a few days which he revealed to Y and offered them all free of cost to the latter. The fear was too contagious that Y declined the offer and one fine morning, before day break the books were abandoned under a mango tree. As an excuse or justification for his actions he put forward the philosophy that, "I don't think it necessary to pass the examination. After all what are the gains of passing the examination? More responsibilities and a transfer to another city on the pretext of lack of vacancies here. And are we losing anything by discarding the examination? Not at all. As a matter of fact, there is no scope or provision for any reduction in our present emoluments on account of non-clearance of the examination." Y too couldn't withstand the verbosity that he too subscribed to the idea and developed a hesitation towards appearing the examination and seeking a promotion.

In the current of time and flow of so many waters under the bridge X was posted on request to his home city, where he got married and lived with his wife and child.

The soulless creatures standing on either side of the road withdrew their eyes, the strangers as they were, dissolved in the evening rush of buses bound for east and west.

THE BRIDGE

Once upon a time there was no bridge connecting the village Melmuri with the outer world. Public transport mode were bus and train. The nearest motorable road was two kilometers away connecting the towns Pattambi and Valanchery and the nearest railway station at Pattambi, ten kilometers afar. Buses plied between the towns only once in a blue Moon. Boarding a bus was no mean task for the people of the village as it involved the barefoot people as they were then, to walk the length and breadth of the distance along paddy fields and marshy mazes and cross a fordable stream. Yes! most of the people as a matter of fact either could not afford or owing to the prevailing social development index could not conceive the idea of chappals. For a very long period people walked to the bus stop called" Advocate gate" if and only if they found it necessary and unavoidable to board a bus and on their return, journey disembarked there itself to walk back home. Still there remained a community of daily commuters comprising a few college students and government employees for whom it proved a daunting task to get inside a bus during the peak hours. There were two private buses one at 8.30 a.m. by which a student can travel to the government college at Pattambi paying the concessional rate of 25 paise, and another bus at 8.45 by which a student can travel only up to a distant bus stop for the college on a parallel road leading to Palakkad paying 20 paise. At 9 a.m. came a red bus with the insignia of an elephant running to Palakkad, owned by Kerala government which gave no concession to students, rarely stopped there. Whether to stop or not was decided by the mood of the crew and not the plight of the travelling public or the probable earnings. In the case of the government operated buses an aversion to take passengers in excess of the sitting capacity was palpable. Most of the private buses were owned by Mayil Vahanam Motors. There were days when they missed buses which passed without sopping there. On such occasions the hapless students had to walk fifteen minutes to the nearest road junction at Koppam to catch any bus coming from another route.

When the incidence of "missing buses" became recurrent it reached the ears of comrade EKS, a shop keeper a few meters ahead of the bus stop. He was forty years old, six feet height, masculine, a self-styled communist theoretician, sporting a mustache like that of Fidel Castro and well-read and up dated about international politics and developments all over the world. Still, he was not a member or follower of any political party. When he came to know about the students and general public being taken for a ride by the bus operators, he did not have to think twice to question them. He began to put barricades on the road to block the erring buses and succeeded in bringing them into line. It had the unexpected fall out of shifting the bus stop from Advocate gate to the new point in front of EKS's shop. Thus, the origin of the bus stop" VIETNAM GATE ".

Vietnam gate happened to be closer to the stream when compared to the old bus stop, the hundred meters distance included a stretch of paddy field and a narrow pathway bordered by shrubs on either side. When people continued their walk between Melmuri and Vietnam Gate, on the days following they felt a considerable reduction in distance. A demand for a bridge was in the air for the past many years which remined a dream unfulfilled for want of a god father. The election for the Kerala assembly in 1970 was a golden opportunity to raise their demand when two stalwarts were in the fray from there. One, the ex-chief minister EMS and the other E.P.Gopalan contesting as candidates of Left Democratic front and United Democratic Front respectively. While EMS responded the demand with a wry smile the other leader commented, "you want electricity, you want bridge.... how such things will materialize...will they come down from the sky?". With out any clue to what the leaders meant their eyes turned towards the sky anticipating the arrival of a bridge, they could see the lightning there followed by the thunder. EMS won the election but could not become the chief minister.

Ten long years passed, so many feet crossed the stream, so many waters flowed through the stream and nobody came from the heaven with a bridge. One day a young man working in a gulf country came on leave with an inflatable boat. He ferried all but the hydrophobics to both sides of the stream free of any service charge. Before returning to his work abroad, he brought two trunks of coconut tree and laid them as a bridge across the stream. The sceptics initially called him crazy and mad found it convenient to cross the stream only later.

By the end of November, the monsoon withdrew and water level gradually receded in the stream and alarm bells rang for the paddy farmers. They had to preserve the water until the seedlings planted during the second season is harvested for which they made a bund using the locally available waste wood, grass and other vegetation. Water filled in much to the muse of farmers and the people living in the neighbor-hood who bathed and washed their cloths on either side of the check dam. Reetha, living on the Melmuri-side of the stream had been tempted by the water for many days, but dared not to enter the water for the fear of being watched by the passersby. However, at a far end of the dam she found a point where she could step in the water, wash her cloths and take a topless bath. On a midday, before lunch, after completing the necessary house hold chores she went to the water to measure its depth and found it more than knee level and took a few more steps to the middle of the stream where the water immersed her loins. She looked around. There was nobody in the vicinity. She stripped off her clothes already soaked in the water surrounding her waist line and held them pressed under the left arm pit and unloosed the hooks of the blouse and bra and had a full view of her breasts in the scintillating sun of November. She looked up at the sky and saw the sun which did not hurt her but was smiling at her. Then she held her palms together with the ten fingers pressing each other, so as to form a bowl and dipped it in water and splashed the water upwards repeatedly. The water falling down found its path from her forehead down the closed eyes, cheeks, neck, shoulders and escaped as a stream between the breasts. She did it for some time as a ritual to Sun-God and whipped out the already let loose blouse and bra to make them into a ball with the clothes kept under the arm pit. The ball was then taken to the shore for soaking with soap, washing and wringing. Meanwhile she too underwent the ablution and swam a few rounds. This became a routine.

One day on the other side of the stream appeared a stranger on a four wheeled wooden plank, a roamer never seen before in the area. Though his legs were week to support his body, a full-grown masculinity and spirit of adventure led him to places after places on his self-invented crutches. He struggled to make his way along the embankment of the stream to see the water, but though he reached near the water he could not see it as his eyes were struck on the magnificent nudity of a woman he had never seen before. He was awe struck looking at the gentle measured movement of her body and the fingers engaged in frequent gentle strokes with soaped cloths on a stone and the rhythmic motion of her breasts with the finger movements. She completed her course of activities in water and left the place.

Rajan felt devastated. He repented about the lost opportunity to have some leisure with the woman at least by way of small talks. But he could not step in the water or jump in from the crutches and swim towards her. He cursed himself and the stars for being an unfortunate exemption unable to walk or swim. That night he could not sleep not because of any remorse about the lost opportunity or subjected to some amoral thoughts but was under a spell of shame. A spell of shame for his own shameful and un mannered look at the naked woman. At the same time an assuaging thought came to him that he was helpless in front of that magnificent sculpture. Had it been a woman one would only have peeped at her and would not dare a straight look even if remaining exposed under the sky. Now he remembered one more thing that fortunately the woman had never seen him or found him out all the while he had been absorbed in that beauty. She would have noticed him had she been animate but how can a sculpture, his thoughts travelled endless to end up in a decision to visit the spot again the next day. What happened yesterday was not a wild dream, he told himself on spotting her at the same point next day. Wanting to catch her attention somehow, he threw a pebble at the water near her which sounded "glum" in the water but she ignored it. He continued the game with pebbles until being caught red handed. She wrathfully swam towards him forgetting her nakedness to get into an altercation. The mount of rage simmering inside her began to thaw at the moment she realizes that he is crippled and offers any help he needs. His wish of many past days fulfills when she lifts him from the crutches to bathe him as if he was a baby. His first bath in the water.

Another generation of leaders were coming up. M.P.Gangadharan was one among them who had close connections with the local Congress leader Rajan Menon staying at Vietnam Gate. One fine morning they starts on foot from Vietnam Gate, crosses the stream to visit Melmuri where they meet the school head master, Karunakaran Nambiar, a follower of congress. In the next election to the Kerala Assembly Gangadharan gets elected to the assembly and becomes the irrigation minister. The irrigation department plans a check dam cum bridge for the stream and executed it. When the minister inaugurated it by cutting the ribbon stretched from one end of the bridge to the other end, a man on crutches crossed the bridge towards Melmuri followed by a woman with a baby in her arms.

THE ISLAND OF NEUROTICS

Francis Narona was on an idle and leisurely walk on the street near his residence. Far away from fifty metres ahead, his eyes spotted Dakshayani one of his ex-office staff approaching with dancing steps, her idiosyncratic movement. In fact, it was not merely a seeing but an exchange of certain emotions between four eyes comprising a feeling of fear, contempt or scorn, or rather a mixture of the three. It was certain, romance had no place there. However, in the evening rush of pedestrians and vehicles it dismayed him, the instantaneous disappearance into oblivion of the soul and body bearing the two eyes. “Perhaps in order to avoid him, she has stepped sideways to the nearby bank complex which also houses a medical store”, he thought and walked ahead with a sigh of relief. Or else she would have taken him as a spirit of the person she had cursed to attain premature death a few years back. She was very confident then of her capacity to curse someone to death and had quoted as instance the death of another of her adversaries.

The next occasion he chanced to see her was a small inaugural function in the neighborhood. He could locate her sitting among other ladies. Such functions were gradually being incepted after the lifting of shut downs and restrictions in the post covid era. He tried to reach out by way of some intentional strides circumventing the sitting ladies, only to catch her attention and exchange pleasantries. But she was staring at something far away perhaps with blank eyes or deliberately to avoid him. Anyway, she was not pleased to see him. Perhaps this time too she might have taken him as the spirit and out of fear stared out blank. Hence, he moved away to another area where he found a vacant chair next to Vinayakan, Dakshayani's husband. Vinayakan was cordial as usual to get along with Francis. When the function was almost over Dakshayani left the chair on which she had been sitting and went straight to her husband. Now as if it is confirmed that it is not a spirit but a real human being talking to her husband, she smiled at him and began to clear some doubts about public transport system after the lifting of restrictions on travel. She had no qualms about her demeanor shown a few minutes back nor had Francis any astonishment about it. He took it as her natural behavior. Moreover, why should a person in need worry about such delicacies? He cleared her doubts as he would have done in any other occasion with any other person. The only question remained was, which came first in her mind, whether the doubts about post covid travel facilities or the urge to accompany her husband home after the function.

While in service his relationship with her as the immediate superior was like a roller coaster drive. For his attitude of treating issues whether official or unofficial based on their merits, they being right or wrong, without giving any emotional tint or explanation to assuage the baseless feelings of others, or to justify his stand did not tread well with her. He can't hear what anybody else has to say, he simply can't. Her penchant for a prolonged discourse though bereft of facts would be set free by then to hit his deaf ears. More than whatever vomited, the portion retained in a cesspool would be released in proper breadth and length, volume and mass and distributed subsequently to others also in a covert, behind the door manner. Perhaps out of distress and melancholy once she dumped a pile of such stuff on Mrs. Francis also who was working in the same office. For Dakshayani this was the third and final charge of ammunition. In the first stage she had directly attacked the enemy ending it with a curse to the death of the enemy, a perfect annihilation. She quoted an instance of sending another person to the grave yard simply through her curse.

Before marriage Francis had lived his life as private individual matters of no concern to anyone else and carried out his official responsibilities as strictly official without any fear or favour and beyond the unnecessary intervention of others. That was his idea of life also. Except for the sense of justice and truth no force on earth could influence his decisions whether friends or relatives or even superiors. His only concern was that his words and actions must be acceptable to God. And he never wasted his time to convince others his righteousness. He had a rare gift in the form of a capacity to ignore anything told behind him whether good or bad and maintaining the equanimity of mind. Everything took a different turn after marriage as it occurred to him. Now the external world gradually began to press him from all sides not directly but through his wife, a pressure which tried to tore apart his soul. Previously nobody was concerned about his morning cup of tea, his breakfast, lunch or dinner. But now the world has begun to show more interest about such banalities seemingly a new interest as far as he is concerned apparently for the sake of a talk which in most occasions were only a small talk with her. Though he was not bothered about such things, sometimes they ended up in sarcastic comments as in the case of a breakfast with rice gruel in a world which held it as something inferior. To peep into the lives of others can be merely an attitude of the small minds but at times it may raise itself to higher levels like questions regarding financial management. Thus, someone asked a question, who is managing the domestic finance, as for them together income also is double? The questioner was happy and satisfied with her reply that both of them are illiterate in that aspect. Later when she shared the story with his father, he made a correction, my son knows it very well but in your case that may be correct.

The filthy mass dumped by Dakshayani on the psyche of Mrs.Francis was her calculated dose which would work as slow poisoning, a snake bite on the finger tip of any of the foot, the poison spreading gradually through the veins. It would radiate from the body as anger against her spouse not affecting anyone else and never kills her. In the height of the torment the couple would not speak each other, not even see eye to eye but melt them down internally. By the evening train the Francis couple had to travel to the neighbouring city. They proceeded to the station walking together speechless, entered the train speechless, lied down on their berths speechless and they never slept because they could not say goodnight. They were melting internally.

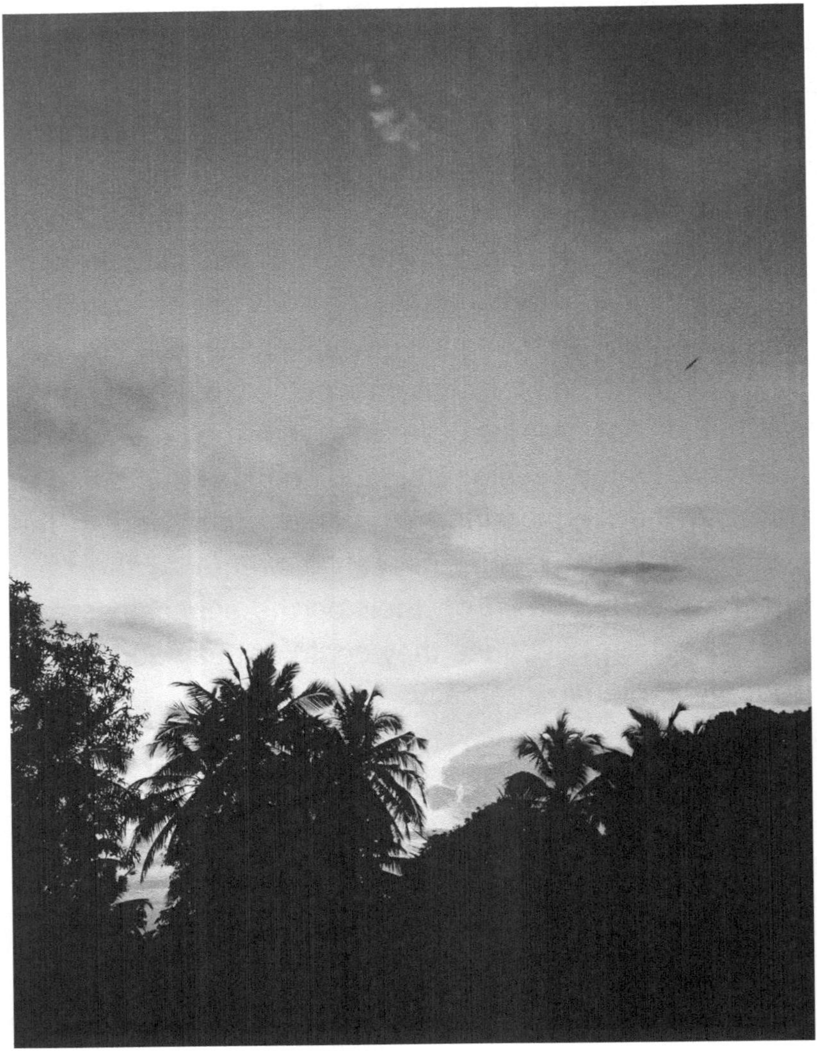

THE FALL OF A KING

Nambiar was not a king but the people of the village just because of his having that much landed property equated him to a king. He lived in a mansion with his two daughters and their family. The daughter's had husbands who were siblings also. Moreover, these brothers were born to his sister; his nephews, sororal nephews to be precise. The matrilineal knot. He was a widower for whom the wife left behind six sons and three daughters before her departure to heavenly abode. Previously they were living in a smaller house but subsequent to the expansion of family by the birth of more children the necessity arose for the construction of a new and larger one. The front portion of the old one was already custom made for a grocery shop. His eldest son TN was in charge of the grocery shop. Second son KN was in charge of all agricultural and farming activities. Third was a daughter married to a central government official working in Tamil Nadu, staying with him there. Fourth, son named PN took charge of agricultural, farming and management of all sundry miscellaneous activity's consequent to the premature demise of KN, the second son. His preference for an independent life not necessarily financial prompted him to move to his own house after marriage. No eye brows were raised about the resources for such an acquisition. KN also had acquired a small house cum shopping centre and an acre of land which was not yet lived in till his death. Fifth, son KSN was working for the Konkan power corporation in Karnataka. Next progeny the daughter named SA continued to stay with father even after her marriage with PPN, her father's nephew who too chose to stay with them. The seventh, son named AN became an outcast in the family because of debauchery and his relationship and marriage with a woman from a lower caste. Born as number eight and youngest daughter KA also was married by her father's nephew PPKN, younger brother of PPN. After the marriage this new groom also found pleasure to stay in wife's house like his brother. He was the head master of the local primary school. By this time brother had taken over the grocery shop from TN. TN had been unceremoniously kicked out from the family after continued feud with father. He found refuge in his wife's house in the village Ponmudi a few kilometres away. The nineth and last member of the family, KVS worked as a technician in a European company in the capital of Tamil Nadu.

The king lived in his mansion peacefully with his two daughters, their husbands and grandchildren. By the couple SA and PPN six and by KA and PPKN three.

They never experienced poverty and did not know what it does mean at a time when the whole state Kerala reeled under famine and the minister in charge of food Paul P Mani travelled in despair to neighbouring states, Tamil Nadu, Andhra Pradesh and Karnataka to procure rice and shuttled often to New Delhi for negotiation with central government for the release of rice and wheat from central pool. Though rice was the stapple food people were compelled to buy wheat also through ration shops as the government could not supply sufficient rice. To fill the stomach dry chunks of tapioca also were available in markets. Wheat was available to anybody from the ration shop irrespective of financial status. Just for variety and quest for a different flavour often grandchildren of Nambiar procured it withstanding the sarcastic comment of the ration dealer Govindan Ezhuttachan," Oh! Nambiar's granary may have become empty". They pounded the wheat to remove the husk and cooked it and mixed with coconut kernel and relished. Even after measuring out the statutory leavy to government the granaries of Nambiar borne a good storage of paddy. As this was not a secret, laborers working for Nambiar at the end of a day's work would hesitate to receive wages in cash but would insist for paddy instead. Their version for this was," one cannot boil and eat the currency note to satisfy the hunger." In addition to paddy, vegetables, fruits and coconut were cultivated and coconut oil and gingelly oil produced. Other house hold provisions only should come from outside. This happened through three channels, one by the occasional supply by the shopkeeper himself, second and third by a regular purchase by the shopkeeper's father-in-law and brother. Life went on smooth inside and outside the house without even a minor irritant between the inmates much to the envy of not only the villagers but the other siblings of the Nair sisters and Nambiar brothers. Here SA and KA are the Nair sisters; PPN and PPKN are the Nambiar brothers.

The grocery shop of PPN the only one in the area, had a history of many years of prosperity and a reputation for the quality of goods sold. The decline in business started with the advent of another shop a few metres away by TGN in the shopping centre left behind by his deceased father KN. The liberal and flexible nature of the young man may have won the hearts of customers, where the adamant old ethos failed. The tea shop in the shopping centre added more to the chagrin of the customers. The decline in business gave him a strong reason to pull the shutters down though the naysayers sensed some other intention behind it. He had already shrugged off suggestions from well-wishers to shift his wife and children to the house adjoining the shop and lead an independent life, years back. However, beware of burglary in the shop he used to stay alone as a night watchman in the upstairs bedroom of the building and join the family at day break for the morning tea. After the breakfast he will proceed to the shop, close it for lunch break, have the lunch and a brief siesta and again to the shop for the busy evening hours in the light of a petromax as the village was not electrified. Villages without electricity depended on oil lamps for lighting and habitually went asleep early at night. The one and only deviation from this general rule was his shop which remained open until the grocery bill of the last customer was settled. Then he will proceed to home with the petromax in one hand and a torch in the other. During the brisk evening hours often his school going son also will be at the shop to help him.

Pulling down the shutters of the shop for ever PPN surrendered the keys of the building under the feet of his uncle and father-in-law, Nambiar who mildly rebuked him reminding that, "of your four girls two are still waiting a wed lock and two sons are continuing their education." One late evening in the dim light of the oil lamp Nambiar was taking bath in the open bath room adjoining the well and extended to the veranda. Though ninety-two years old he used to dab his body with an ayurvedic oil daily and wash it off with soap and warm water sitting on a wooden seat laid on the bath room floor. That night he repeatedly called out the names of his two daughters, the voice failed to reach the ears tangled in the hustle bustle of the kitchen but it had reached the ears of his second son-in-law PPKN. Sensing some danger, he rushed to the bath room and prevented his uncle from falling to ground who had started leaning to one side. It was a stroke. The doctor from the primary health centre was brought in who confirmed the stroke and forecast a coma of twenty-four hours before his last breath. By this time his son PN had already taken charge of the affairs and many people from the neighbour hood thronged in the veranda including the outcast AN. Next morning the number of people increased with the arrival of more, dear and near ones including the eldest son TN and his available sons. Lunch was served for all those present and by evening the son from Karnataka and his wife arrived. It happened as forecast by the doctor. The youngest son reached there by the morning train, next day morning.

Life after death would be an enigmatic question but Nambiar had already answered the questions about what to do about his mortal remains. The burial site of his wife had been kept as a monument built of laterite stone and cement, of length eight feet, width two feet and a projection of two feet above the ground with a wire-net cavity for keeping an oil lamp at one end. Adjacent and parallel to the monument he had built an underground pit sufficient in length, depth and width to lay down his body, with an arch shaped canopy for protection from rain and shine. Until now for many years after construction this pit was used to store sand brought from Bharthappuzha for minor works which also became a secluded labor room for stray bitches. Often it was surprising to see a litter of puppies suddenly pacing around the courtyard as the presence of the bitch remained unnoticed so far. Now the sand has been removed and the premises cleared for the burial. Followed by the traditional rites at the courtyard of the mansion the body was taken to the site by a group of pallbearers comprising his sons and grandsons with the exception of his youngest son who supposedly was weary of a night's journey. Young men volunteered to gently place the body inside the cave-like pit had a tough time in the air tight chamber.

There was a mourning period of fifteen days and farewell lunch for the people hanging around during the past many days and invited and uninvited guests on the sixteenth day. Speculations had already started about the future of the mansion and landed properties scattered around the village, in the minds of insiders and outsiders. Outsiders cast their eyes up the sky for any glimpse of fire and smoke coming out of the internal squabbles. Insiders included sons, daughters and grandchildren of the departed including the hopeful and at the same time doubtful excommunicated ones. All were waiting anxiously for the opening of the pandora's box; the document called will supposed to have been left behind by the deceased. And finally, it was opened to the shock and dismay of a few as expected. The ominous omissions were TN and AN, the excommunicated. However, an understanding was reached to assuage the feelings of the excluded also and to avoid any possible legal challenges and to facilitate the smooth registration of post partition documents.

The will had conceived it jointly for the two daughters, SA and KA; two houses with all its encompassing land, wells, ponds, trees, coconut and areca nut cultivations, cattle, etc. Paddy fields were a valuable possession those days when compared with other landed property. All paddy fields also were set apart in their favour. Remaining lands of extensions ranging from two acres to twelve acres with names for each property scattered around the village were shared between others. They shared the money proportionately as all of them were unanimous in the idea to sell the land sans any division or change to the boundaries but changed the titles and ownership in exchange of gulf money.

The king would have dreamed, the brothers, his sons in law will live in peace leading to the eventual spread of the peace and harmony to the sisters and their progeny. But as the two brothers battled viciously for hegemony it became inevitable to avoid further deterioration and damage. PN, KSN, and KVS worked together as a three-member jury to bring about an amicable settlement by apportionment of the property jointly set apart for the sisters. For the parleys and negotiations KSN came from Karnataka and KVS from Chennai. As he felt the need to influence the jury PPN tried his best through the secret one to one meeting and suspected conspiracy with the jury members. It was to his advantage that his eldest daughter was married to the brother-in-law of KVS. Nevertheless, his master stroke happened to be the chicken curry by which he turned KSN in his favour who even dared to declare his allegiance and partiality to SA. The other jury members declared their impartiality and maintained an air of diplomacy. There was an undercurrent and wave of sympathy in favour of PPN and SA taking into account the joblessness of the former and the number of children they have. The jury prepared two tables of properties. The table one comprised the new mansion and the adjoining land of eight acres with pond, areca nut farm etc., and paddy field of two acres. It was rich with very old teak, mango, jackfruit and other varieties of trees also. The table two comprised of the old unused house with adjoining land of one acre, another land of one acre area a few yards away and paddy field of one acre. The abandoned house already had acquired a possessed look with all doors and windows including their frames eaten by white ants. Most of the wooden beams and panels supporting the tiled roofs needed replacement as they had decayed due to exposure to rain waters escaping through the broken tiles. The travesty of justice was palpable in the preparation of the table. But it was sugar coated by laying down a clause for payment of a sum of rupees eight thousand and three hundred by the party enjoying table one to the party taking the items stipulated in table two. Any imbalance or injustice were deemed to be nullified and the only task remained was to persuade KA and family into a mind set to accept the table two. The task was completed successfully by KVS. Meanwhile the only better advise came to KA and family happened to be from the cattle keeper who had suggested them covertly to demand a share of the areca farm also, a vital suggestion which went unheeded. The vitality of a suggestion must inevitably have a bearing on the person making it.

When any deal is struck the next stage is its implementation. Here the implementation means the eviction of PPKN and family from the mansion. The real challenge they faced was "how to move to a dilapidated house." Make it fit for habitation meant money and time. By this time KSN and KVS had returned to their respective work places and PN was the only conduit for communication between the brothers PPN and PPKN. The ball was set rolling by PPN who kicked it to PN for arranging an early shifting by PPKN and family who in turn requested an advance payment for the repairs and renewals from the proposed eight thousand and three hundred rupees. The request was refused outrightly on the pretext that repairs and renewals can be executed subsequent to occupancy of the house. If the situation has any similarity with the partition of India in 1947 and Gandhiji's hunger strike for the early release of 50 crores of rupees to Pakistan as per the partition accord, here nobody came forward with rescue effort. The eyes of KA flooded with tears when the circumstances compelled her to offer the couple of bangles on her hand to raise money for the urgent repairs in the presence of her brother PN and husband PPKN. In the days following the bats and spiders the inhabitants of the past many years were forced to flee, the walls and floors tamped with mud and cow dung, the ghostly doors and windows replaced, the house was ready for consecration.

CORPORATE HOLIDAY

The wound was deep inside the core of his heart. The bottle of whisky he shared with the person who shares his room could not heal it even though he had gulped in the major share while the latter's snores set the back ground score. Instead of the slighting had she stabbed him with a knife he would have been sleeping happily, the eternal sleep.

It was the second edition of their company's holiday camp. While the first one was a family tour this sequel is exclusively for employees. Still that disappointing situation at the beginning of the family tour ruminates in his mind. They as a family; Lenin, Nadiya and two children had already occupied convenient seats in a carriage. Just minutes before, the two carriages engaged for the tour were ready to move, a lady hurried up inside their carriage and looks around searching for a seat and her forlorn eyes comes in contact with those of Nadya. Nadya realizing the lady's predicament peremptorily suggests Lenin to offer his seat to the lady. Lenin vacates his seat and rushes to the other carriage to find a seat. The displeasure and disappointment experienced while breaking away from one's family atmosphere often ruminates in his mind. Being the only couple working for the company it was everybody's pleasure to allow Lenin and Nadiya the privacy they deserved but her refusal to accept the couple suite room without even consulting the husband raised the eyebrows of others with surprise and suspicion against her justification that she dislikes any special consideration. Thus, the couple got decoupled that night with the lady sharing a suite with some other women of her choice and he being allotted a room with another man. For her there was something feminine in the bottom of her mind which declared independence that night. The sarcastic comments to which Lenin was exposed on account of that belittlement was not a matter of her concern and rather than dying down, the comments created ripples in his mind. He drifted along the crests and troughs of the ripples with a byline in his mind, "It's a dangerous thing to domesticate even horses, let alone women." He felt clueless about the source of the byline even after scratching the head for a long time.

Whether it is a boon or bane, Nadiya had an inherent quality to express her observations and thoughts as they first came to her mind at any given situation without losing its freshness and clarity. Though Lenin had initially ignored this attitude as just an impulsive nature gradually he felt it as disappointing and irritating, but surprisingly, he could not respond or retort. Something from a remote corner of his mind constrained him or restrained him or rather a state of mindlessness had engulfed him of which he was not aware. He could always recall unostentatiously, an experience when on their first date he gave order for two orange juices in good faith and camaraderie. But as though underlining or establishing her ego, worth, will or individuality or something which is better known to her only, she quickly intervenes to amend, as one orange and one sweet lime. However, after a few sips she moved the glass aside and relished the orange juice as she found the sweet lime juice rather pungent despite its nomenclature. Even if far away from truth, the confidence, clarity, tone, intensity, an element of entertainment and authority with which an idea is delivered makes it something more than a universal truth. (After all who is bothered about the truth). So, the audience as a group or individual as the case may be will be hell bent to accept and heed it as if they have lost their discretion. Rather than the perplexities of the vice the assertiveness of the wicked is the order of the day and it inevitably rules the roost. On the other hand, nature had made Lenin so generous to suffer everything silently as an innocent victim. But her manner of taking a decision on any matter or the way to handle a situation had no relationship with what she expressed generally and remained contrary to her aforesaid postures. She had a natural propensity to ensure that proper consideration has been given to the aspect, "what others may think", about her words, actions and demeanor, in any situation which ultimately became the quintessence of her success story as a social being. The obsession about "what others may think" always carried with it an unexpected dividend, an entry in the good books of others. Further the attitude of a socialist seemed natural in her sense of equality with all living things and she was deft in maintaining an emotional rapport with people of all ages whether younger or elder to her irrespective of sex. As a testimony to this Nadiya had narrated an anecdote to Lenin during the initial days of their marriage. According to her the incident happened in Tiruchchirappalli, her home town, during the last phase of her school days, to be precise while she was a higher secondary student. Then her family, parents and two children, where staying as tenants on the upstairs of an old two-story building, the landlord's family stay put ground floor.

The landlord a Tamil Brahmin, his wife and daughter Kasturi a college dropout was staying there. Of their two sons the elder one was working in U.S and the other one in Mumbai. Though Kasturi was elder to Nadiya at least by ten years she could easily wipe out the barriers of age by her very sense of equality and they became friends daring to share issues related to their private life. Thus, she becomes privy to the knowledge that Kasturi is a married woman whose husband is an army officer, but Kasturi kept a tactful silence about further details of her family life. But Kasturi often sought her company to visit a physician whom Kasturi claimed as her family physician whose name board revealed that he was practicing psychiatry. Though Nadiya resisted herself from asking any offensive question about Kasturi's psychic condition she felt the whole affair clandestine. Once during their journey back from the psychiatrist's clinic Kasturi revealed that at times she would be under the fire of passion which would lead her to the doctor for extinguishing the fire who deftly absorbs the fire giving her the ultimate bliss. Nadiya's camaraderie with Kasturi as the most confident escort for the day light adultery continued as and when the latter desired to the satisfaction of her lust until Nadiya's marriage but what she lamented most was Kasturi may be feeling rudderless due to her absence. When her narration was complete, Lenin became spellbound and commented, "after your marriage and relocation to Chennai."

"Yes, after my marriage and relocation from Trichy she must be at loss of a friend to whom she could confide the feelings in her soul." Nadiya replied.

"Rather than the loss of friendship it must be the craving for an appointment with the psychiatrist, tormenting her Perdita", retorted Lenin.

What dismayed Lenin much was her audacity to solace Kasturi even in the time of the filthy moral abasement.

The culmination of the holiday camp was like an awakening from an extended dream for everyone except

Lenin who could neither sleep nor dream. On their way back Nadiya proudly introduced another lady with a hand full of liquor bottles, "my friend Anitha, her husband could not make it for this tour as he is not our company staff but to compensate, she has purchased all these stuff for him." Lenin shook hands with the lady and joined a chorus with her to say that," but we are not strangers." He added that he was fortunate to occupy a seat beside her during the first tour and the warm friendship continues. Nadiya looked into their eyes with an air of suspicion and tried to smile.

THE JOURNEY BEGINS

The journey begins. James Philip (JP) is in search of Nancy Stoks. Until his incredible connection with her through the OTT platform one hour before, she would have been nobody to him. For the past one hour during the sleepless night, he was brain storming himself on various aspects of the film, "GOOD LUCK TO YOU, LEO GRANDE". Living on the peninsular southern end of India he could not first of all, digest Nancy's liaison with the twenty-year-old gigolo at first. The adventures of the sixty-four-year-old retired teacher after the death of her husband remained unplacated in a remote corner of his mind. This was an addition to a similar enigma sprouted in his mind when reports about the marriage of Emmanuel Macron with his teacher came out through media. In each case he observed the tendency of his mind to slip easily from their cultural moorings to the physiological inevitabilities and intricacies. Any perception of an upper hand of emotional bondage in such cases may very well be open to dispute even by sexologists or psychologists of the range of Sigmund Froid or Abraham Maslow.

The night had in its stock pile all the tyrannies and turmoil of world to greet JP after his sojourn of three months. So far, the river was flowing flaw less. But that night he experienced the unusual turbulence, violence and blockades on her path which should have flowed taking him also along with her, sharing the orgies and ecstasies and finally merge and dissolve in the ocean. He was quick to realize that the river is going through the inevitable phase of drying. From the pangs of the drying river, he too could not escape and was subjected to its fury. In spite of all his attempts to caress, cajole and arouse the river to ecstasy she rejected him and appeared intimidating. Un able to withstand the fury of drying river he withdrew to a safe zone dejected and sleepless, beyond the vicinity of the river.

The sleepless night kindles his thoughts. Distraught as he was and devoid of sleep JP opens wide, the door of his book shelf and surveys the titles to select one. His eyes pounce upon one recent addition to the shelf and takes it out. He glances through the biography of the harlot, a book well received and discussed by the society supposedly due to its pioneerdom in that regional language. Apart from the content he frantically searched for her phone number, an effort proved in vain. Of course, her life would have been in peril had she mentioned her phone number in the book, he told himself. It was not lust or passion but a craving for love, a motherly love which only women would be capable of, the factor leading him that moment. He wanted to communicate with her, open up his mind and share his feelings. Having nothing else to do he flip flopped the pages of the book hesitantly. Though he vacillated through some more books but could not focus his mind. He yearned to look into eyes that are conciliating and radiating love, wished a mellifluous voice befall his ears. He remembered the college days sharing an accommodation with friends, Madhavan, EMP, Philip Sabu and Jorry Mathew where the cuisine was looked after by the middle-aged Madhavi Amma. She looked after, not only the kitchen but the youngsters also with a motherly affection. Perhaps every mother has deep inside her the acumen of a psychologist irrespective of she being a literate or illiterate. She proved it once when he was left alone with Madhavi Amma and friends being left for their villages. She had already identified a sort of melancholy in JP which she thought could be set right by the company of a girlfriend. So, without asking or discussing the issue with him she brought two girls to make him happy. Though they stayed there for two days he ignored them as he was not prepared in mind to lose his virginity. When his friends returned, Madhavi Amma never betrayed a hint but the gossip had its run around the neighborhood. Now with the book "ONE HUNDRED YEARS OF SOLITUDE "on his hands he forayed into the life of the character, Pilar Ternera. In his first reading of the book, he had discovered the towering presence of the woman character Ursula as wife, mother, grandmother, great grandmother and more to the list and an ominous situation in which she follows a trickle of blood reaching the kitchen where she was working. From the kitchen she follows the trail of blood along the fathomless mazes to reach a house, inside of which she finds her son Jose Arcadio lying in a pool of blood. JP found the situation thrilling, and had exclaimed then, "oh! Lordy, blood in search of blood." The second reading present before him a Pilar Ternera an apostle of love, recused of the image of a promiscuous woman.

Ensuring that all the books taken out from the shelf are kept back on the rakes properly he tried his luck on the laptop where he huddles with the movie," GOOD LUCK TO YOU, LEO GRANDE". Watching the movie, he becomes completely devastated initially but gradually recovers to the extent of forming in his mind some messages for Nancy. He kept it close to his heart. But there is no meaning in keeping it to himself, knowledge should be transferred. So, he decides to pass the message to Nancy, the retired teacher. He knew it would be no mean task to teach a teacher about a river drying up, the pangs of which one should inevitably under go and experience. If the river denies to have experienced that pangs, she must have been dreaming. He wanted to woke Nancy up from the dream, from her dream of adventures with Leo Grante, bring her to the world of reality with her eyes opened wide, love flowing from them incessantly.

Night was conspiring with day about handing over the torch. Through the darkness JP moved out of his house, gently closed the doors behind him and begins the journey in search of Nancy Stoks.